First published by Parragon in 2010

Parragon
Queen Street House
4 Queen Street
Bath BA1 1HE, UK

Copyright © Parragon Books Ltd 2009
Design by Pink Creative Ltd

ISBN: 978-1-4075-8641-0

Printed in China

# A Dog's Life

inspiration for dog lovers everywhere

Bath · New York · Singapore · Hong Kong · Cologne · Delhi · Melbourne

# A dog is man's best friend.

Unknown

# Dogs are
## miracles

# with paws.

Susan Ariel Rainbow Kennedy (Attrib), Author

# A good dog
## deserves
### a good bone. American proverb

The reason a dog has

so many friends

is that he

wags his tail

instead of his tongue.

Unknown

There is
no psychiatrist in the world

like a
puppy

licking your face. Bern Williams, Author

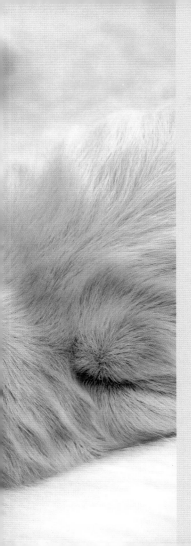

The
biggest
dog
has been a
pup.

Joaquin Miller, Poet

# A dog
## is one of the remaining
# reasons

why some people can be persuaded

to go for a walk.

OA Battista, Author

My little dog -

a heartbeat

at my feet.

Edith Wharton, Novelist

Dogs are not our

whole life,

but they make

lives whole.

Roger Caras, Wildlife photographer

# If your dog doesn't

like someone

you
probably
shouldn't
either. Unknown

To **live** long,

**eat** like a **cat**,

drink

like a dog. German proverb

Dogs feel very **strongly** that they should always go with you in the $car,$

in case the need should arise for them to **bark** nothing right in your $ear.$

Dave Barry, Columnist

# A door

is what a dog is

perpetually on the
wrong side of.

Ogden Nash, Poet

If you can look
at a dog and not feel

vicarious
excitement

and affection,

you must be a cat.

Unknown

# Anybody

who doesn't know what soap

## tastes like

## has never

## washed a dog.

Franklin P Jones, Businessman

# The dog was created specially for children.

He is the god of frolic.

Henry Ward Beecher, Clergyman

Yesterday I was a dog.
Today I'm a dog.
Tomorrow I'll probably

still be a dog.
Sigh!

There's so little hope for
advancement.

Charles M Schulz, Cartoonist

# Don't accept

your dog's admiration
as conclusive evidence
that you are wonderful.

Ann Landers, Columnist

My goal in life is to be as good as my dog already thinks I am.

Unknown

a person

41

No matter how little money

having a dog makes

and how few possessions you own,
you rich.

Louis Sabin, Author

The **cat** will mew

and the **dog** will have

his day.

William Shakespeare, Poet and playwright

It is nought good a sleeping hound wake.

Geoffrey Chaucer, Author and poet

Dogs are better
than human beings
because they know
but do not tell.

Unknown

49

A puppy is but a dog,

plus

high spirits,

and

minus

common sense.

Agnes Repplier, Essayist

# Every dog is a lion at home.

HG Bohn, Publisher

# Dachshund:
a half-a-dog high
and a
dog-and-a-half long.

Henry Louis Mencken, Journalist

The **difference**
between cats and dogs is,

dogs come

when they are called,

cats take a message

and get back to you.

Unknown

# Man

is a dog's idea

of what God should be.

Holbrook Jackson, Journalist

There is no faith which has never been broken, except that of a truly

# faithful dog.

Konrad Lorenz, Zoologist

One reason
a dog can be such a comfort
when you're feeling blue

is that he doesn't try
to find out why.

Unknown

Properly trained, a man can be a dog's best friend.

Corey Ford, Humorist and author

When a dog wants to hang out the

## "Do Not Disturb"

sign, as all of us do now and then, he is regarded as a

# traitor

to his species.

Ramona C Albert

# The most affectionate creature in the world is a wet dog.

Ambrose Bierce, Journalist

Life is like a dog sled team.

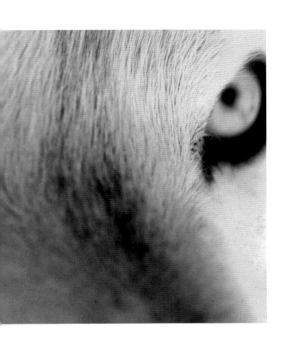

If you ain't the lead dog,

the scenery never changes.

Lewis Grizzard, Writer

If you stop every time a dog barks, your road will never end.

Saudi Arabian proverb

Women and cats will

do as they please,

and men and dogs should

relax

and get used to it.

Robert A. Heinlein, Novelist

No one appreciates the very special genius of your conversation as the dog does.

Christopher Morley, Journalist

Did you ever **walk** into a room and forget why you walked in?

I think that is how dogs **spend** their lives.

Sue Murphy

A dog can express more with his tail in seconds than his owner can express with his tongue in hours.

Unknown

# A dog has the soul of a philosopher.

Plato, Philosopher

You can tell by the
**kindness** of a dog
how a **human**
should be.

Don van Vliet, Musician

You can run
with the big dogs
or sit on the porch
and bark.

Unknown

A dog is the
**only thing**
on earth
that loves you
more than he loves
**himself.**

Josh Billings, Writer and humorist

A dog owns nothing,
yet is seldom
dissatisfied.

Irish proverb

I've seen a look in dogs' eyes, a quickly vanishing look of amazed contempt, and I am convinced that basically dogs think humans are nuts.

John Steinbeck, Writer

Every dog has **his day** but the **nights** are reserved for the cats.

Unknown

# Picture credits